D0065500

_____

_____

_____

_____

_____

TRUTHS FOR LIFE

JIM BERG

WHEN
TROUBLE
COMES

BJU PRESS

GREENVILLE, SOUTH CAROLINA

Library of Congress Cataloging-in-Publication Data

Berg, Jim, 1952-
    When trouble comes / Jim Berg.
        p. cm.
    ISBN 1-57924-812-8 (hardcover : alk. paper)
    1. Suffering--Religious aspects--Christianity. I. Title.
    BV4909 B47 2002
    248.8´.6--dc21

                                        2002001075

Cover image by PhotoDisc, Inc.

NOTE: The fact that materials produced by other publishers may be referred to in this volume does not constitute an endorsement by Bob Jones University Press of the content or theological position of materials produced by such publishers. The position of Bob Jones University Press, and the University itself, is well known. Any references and ancillary materials are listed as an aid to the student or the teacher an in an attempt to maintain the accepted academic standards of the publishing industry.

All Scripture is quoted from the Authorized King James Version.

When Trouble Comes
Jim Berg

Design by Brannon McAllister
Composition by Kelley Moore

© 2002 by Bob Jones University Press
Greenville, South Carolina 29614

BJU Press grants the original purchaser a limited license to reproduce the Help Card for personal use.

Printed in the United States of America

ISBN 1-57924-812-8

15   14   13   12   11   10   9   8   7   6   5   4   3   2   1

DEDICATION

On September 11, 2001, America was attacked by Islamic terrorists. On that fateful day thousands lost their lives at the World Trade Center in New York City and the Pentagon in Washington, D.C.

This book is dedicated to the families and friends who lost loved ones on that horrible day. May they find in these brief chapters the hope they need in these troubled times.

TABLE OF CONTENTS

APPENDICES

INTRODUCTION

S ince you are reading this book, you are probably facing a time of trouble—or are trying to help someone else who is currently going through a time of crisis. Or maybe you are seeking to better prepare yourself for the next difficulty that will come your way. If any of these scenarios apply, this book is for you.

While a book this small cannot deal with every problem that can arise in life, it can help you clear up the confusion so that you can see the most important issues. Think of the four truths we will discuss in this book as "emergency procedures." Together they form "spiritual CPR" interventions to get you—or the person you are helping—stabilized.

You can think of these four truths as a "crisis checklist." You may want to memorize them—just as EMS personnel have to memorize certain emergency procedures. These truths are printed together at the end of this book so that you can photocopy them and carry them with you. You may even want to post them in conspicuous places at home or in your car as daily reminders of how to respond to the crises of life.

After you have read through the entire book to gain an overview, read the seven chapters again—perhaps one chapter per day—and answer the "Take Time to Reflect" questions for each chapter, which are printed in the appendices of this book. This additional study will increase the impact of these truths upon your heart.

May God bless you as you learn to apply His truths for times of trouble.

THE CRISIS

T he symbols you see on this page are the Chinese symbols that combine to form our word "crisis." The top symbol represents the word "danger," and the bottom symbol is the word "opportunity." Together they form a very powerful word picture.

Every crisis has within it the possibility of great danger but also brings with it the opportunity for positive change. Our goal in a crisis must be to escape the danger of the situation and seize the opportunities.

A wonderful reality about life under the Creator God is that He can rescue us from the dangers of anger and bitterness, despair and hopelessness, or fear and anxiety. He can

then turn the situation into an opportunity for our good and
for His glory. This is what the apostle Paul was talking about
when he said,

> There hath no temptation taken you but such as is
> common to man: but God is faithful, who will not
> [allow][1] you to be tempted above that ye are able; but
> will with the temptation also make a way to escape, that
> ye may be able to bear it (I Corinthians 10:13).

The word "temptation" means simply a test God sends
to expose something good or bad about a man's heart. Every
test of life—every crisis—has within it a danger that we can
"escape" if we respond wrongly and an opportunity to show
how great God is if we respond correctly.

A CRISIS PRIMER

The Bible is full of instructions for handling hard times.
It presents many accounts of people who suffered. As you
may know, the Old Testament patriarch Job faced many ex-
cruciating problems. In just a few hours he lost his entire
farm—all of his livestock and grain fields. In addition, all of
his children died when the house collapsed on them during

a violent storm. Shortly thereafter, he lost his own health, and his body was covered with painful boils (Job 1:1–2:7).

Life was so difficult that his wife urged him to "curse God and die" (Job 2:9). His friends were not much help either. They tried to convince him that God was trying to judge him for some hidden sin. The facts, however, revealed that Job was more righteous than any other man on the earth. When his suffering did not end, he became very discouraged.

During a conversation with his unhelpful friends, Job said, "Man is born [for] trouble, as the sparks fly upward" (Job 5:7). He realized that just as surely as sparks from a campfire will ascend with the smoke, so a man will surely experience much trouble in his life. By the end of the book that bears his name, Job had learned how to handle his trouble skillfully and joyfully.

Many of the psalms were written by David, the king of Israel, during very difficult times of his life. The prophets in the Bible faced much opposition from their audiences. Even Jesus Christ is called "a man of sorrows, and acquainted with grief" (Isaiah 53:3).

New Testament Christians endured much persecution from the unbelieving world around them. In fact, two whole books of the New Testament—James and I Peter—were written specifically for suffering people. So there is much help for us in the Bible about how to handle times of crisis and suffering.

THE MANY FACES OF TROUBLE

Think with me about the kinds of trouble that come our way today. Trouble comes from many sources and affects us in many ways.

- A husband is diagnosed with terminal cancer. Within months he leaves his wife a widow and his children fatherless.
- An unmarried daughter tells her parents that she is pregnant, and she runs away with her boyfriend.
- A teenage son is arrested for shoplifting and is subsequently expelled from school.
- A wife announces to her husband that she is leaving him for a man at work with whom she has been having an affair.
- A wife discovers that her husband has been heavily involved with internet pornography or that he has been abusing their ten-year-old daughter.

- A young couple loses their first child through a miscarriage. A second child is born two years later but has multiple birth defects, which make his daily life—and the lives of his parents—very difficult.

- A business partner finds that his associate has cheated him out of profits that should have been equally divided between them. The misdeeds were covered by obscure legal language but were, nonetheless, ethically wrong.

- A husband discovers his wife's gambling addiction when all their credit cards have been charged to the limit. She refuses to admit that it is a serious problem and insists that if he were a better provider for the family, the bills would not be a problem.

- A college student, whose father promised to pay for his room, board, and tuition, finds out that his dad has just been laid off from his job. The young man is left with an unexpected debt of thousands of dollars.

- A family that is already financially strapped wakes up one morning to find that their sewer line has backed up, flooding the first floor of their home. The sewer repair bill and replacement floor covering will cost thousands of dollars. Their minimum insurance will not cover the loss.

- A fifty-year-old factory worker is fired from his job for his contentious spirit. His wife and children are quite fearful that he won't be able to get another good job because of a history of poor job performance.

Of course, this list could go on and on. We can easily see from the scenarios above that problems can come in various "flavors." Some of life's problems are temporary; others are permanent. Some problems are caused by other people; other problems are of our own making.

We must realize that each of these troubles has a built-in danger and an accompanying opportunity to watch God at work and to show His greatness to others.

We must also understand that if we respond wrongly to any of these crises, the situation can become even more complicated. Financial problems can increase even more if wrong choices are made. Strained relationships can be further damaged if the parties react in a selfish way. Friends and family members with life-threatening diseases can degenerate further if they refuse to cooperate with their doctors.

So it is important that we accurately diagnose our trouble and respond correctly. Thankfully, God has graciously given us much help for handling trouble the right way. The following chapters will outline the basics for us.

THE TEST OF JOY

As I mentioned before, the New Testament letters of James and I Peter were written to hurting, suffering people. They provide much direction about trouble. One of the first things we see in both books is that it is possible to have great joy in the midst of great trouble. Notice these passages.

> Blessed be the God and Father of our Lord Jesus Christ, which according to his abundant mercy hath [caused us to be born again] unto a [living] hope by the resurrection of Jesus Christ from the dead. . . . [It is in this hope that] ye greatly rejoice, though now for a season, if need be, ye are in heaviness through [various trials] (I Peter 1:3, 6).

> My brethren, count it all joy when ye fall into [various trials]; knowing this, that the trying of your faith worketh patience. But let patience have her [maturing] work, that ye may be [mature] and [complete], wanting nothing (James 1:2-4).

The joy and rejoicing spoken of in these passages is not a giddy silliness in the midst of tragedy. Neither is it the same as having a positive outlook on life. Scriptural joy is the enjoyment and delight that comes from greater intimacy with God Himself in the midst of the sorrow and trouble. It is a direct result of increased fellowship with God. It is called the "fruit of the Spirit" because it is produced within us supernaturally by God's Spirit (Galatians 5:22-23). It is not something we can generate on our own.

The presence or absence of this joy shows us whether we are handling the trial in the proper way. Our example is Jesus Christ, who experienced great delight in doing His Father's will, even though He was physically tortured by crucifixion. The Scriptures say,

> Let us run with patience the race [of life] that is
> set before us, looking unto Jesus the author and fin-
> isher of our faith; who for the joy that was set before
> him endured the cross, despising the shame (Hebrews
> 12:1-2).

He looked forward to the joy of once again being in the Father's "house" awaiting the coming union with His bride, the church, whom He was dying to redeem. That coming day of blessing was a "blessed hope" to Him, as it is to us (Titus 2:13).

Because Jesus Christ endured all of the agonies of living on a fallen planet, He can be our best Comforter when trouble comes. He not only feels the afflictions we are experiencing but is also ready to help us in our time of need. The Bible says,

> For we have not an high priest [speaking of Jesus Christ] which cannot be touched with the feeling of our infirmities; but was in all points tempted like as we are, yet without sin. Let us therefore come boldly [through prayer] unto the throne of grace [where Jesus Christ sits right now in heaven], that we may obtain mercy [forgiveness for our sins], and find grace to help in time of need (Hebrews 4:15-16).

These verses mean that because Jesus Christ experienced every possible problem that we can encounter, He is very sensitive to the difficulties we are experiencing. And since He is a loving God, He will use His power to come to our aid in times of need. He does not promise to deliver us from our negative circumstances, but He does promise to deliver us from the wrong responses—the dangers—that will destroy our joy and obscure His own glory (I Corinthians 10:13).

With these opening thoughts in mind, let's begin by looking at the danger that our trouble can pose to us. What dangers may lurk in our trouble? How can we be rescued from those dangers?

---

[1]Throughout this book all italics are mine unless specifically noted. Anytime words are bracketed in a Scripture text, it means that I have added or substituted some words to further explain the meaning of the verse.

2

THE DANGER

PEGGY'S PROBLEM

Peggy was waiting outside my office when I arrived one morning. Her puffy eyes told me she had been crying quite a bit. She burst into tears as I invited her in and asked her to tell me what was wrong. Peggy proceeded to tell me that the night before she had found evidence on their family computer that her husband, Bill, had been visiting pornographic sites.[1]

She had not spoken to Bill about it yet. She said that ten years ago, shortly after they were first married, she had discovered pornographic magazines in the car trunk and had almost destroyed their marriage by the way she had handled the situation. She didn't want to repeat her failure of a decade ago. Both of them had made significant spiritual progress since that awful time, so this discovery really took her by surprise. She wanted direction about how to make sure that she was responding rightly to God before she approached Bill. Peggy's concern that she have the right response was vitally important.

That brings us to the first truth on our "emergency checklist."

Truth #1: The greatest danger is always the flesh.

The term "flesh" may be unfamiliar to you. The Bible uses the word "flesh" to describe the sinful part of every one of us, which tries to make life work on our own—without God. When a man is living "after the flesh" (Romans 8:5), he is handling life the way *he* wants to handle it, instead of handling life the way *God* wants it handled. The result of such self-centeredness is *always* destructive (Galatians 6:7-8).

DON'T INFECT THE WOUND!

In December 1998 I had quadruple by-pass surgery. As I was wheeled into the operating room, I looked around and saw two workers opening packages of sterilized instruments.

They laid them out carefully on two carts next to the operating table. The anesthesiologist was getting me ready for surgery. All of them wore sterilized surgical gloves, gowns, and masks. Every precaution was being taken to insure that my surgery would not be further complicated by an infection from contaminated instruments and people.

In the same way that contamination infects a wound, a fleshly—selfish—response to any crisis of life further complicates the situation. Peggy was naturally hurt and fearful after discovering her husband's pornographic indulgences on the internet. But she knew that if she responded in self-centered anger and bitterness, she would further alienate her husband and complicate any reconciliation between Bill and God and between Bill and herself.

She, of course, could nag him, treat him with disgust and contempt, or gossip about him to her friends. Or she could ignore his indulgence, hoping it would go away. (In another similar situation, the bitter wife retaliated by running credit cards up to the maximum limit. She reasoned, "If he can have his indulgence, I can have mine!" Her selfish response further complicated the problems in their marriage.)

Peggy knew that she could neither ignore the problem nor attack the problem with "unclean hands." She wanted to be sure she handled it the right way—*God's* way.

The apostle James gives specific instructions for handling suffering. He calls us to self-examination. In James 4:8 he says, *"Cleanse your hands, ye sinners; and purify your hearts, ye double minded."*

Jesus Himself tells us to do some "spiritual lumberjacking" to get the logs out of our own eyes before we try to remove the splinters from other people's eyes (Matthew 7:3-5). The apostle Paul reminds us as well that when people have treated us wrongly we are not to be "overcome [by] evil, but overcome evil with good" (Romans 12:21). We cannot expect to help the situation by pouring more evil into an already "nasty stew." If we do so, we can make it only worse.

If we do handle the situation with "unclean hands," we can expect that the "infection" will produce a "fever." Certain symptoms reveal that our heart has been contaminated by the flesh. They include the things we have already noticed as danger signs:

- anger and bitterness
- despair and hopelessness
- fear and anxiety

They can be avoided entirely if the situation is handled properly at the beginning. If they arise, they can be remedied by following the plan outlined in the next two chapters.

THE GREATEST DANGER

The greatest manifestation of the flesh is the familiar toxin of *stubbornness*. Nothing will pollute a situation faster than a stubborn will. It is exactly the opposite of the humility of Jesus Christ. Though His earthly circumstances included rejection, ridicule, misunderstanding, torture, and eventually death, Jesus Christ submitted to His Father's will for Him. He was *never* stubborn.

Stubbornness is the greatest hindrance to Christian growth. In fact, the apostle Peter said that "God [fights against] the [stubborn], but gives [divine help] to the humble" (I Peter 5:5).

In Luke 8, Jesus compares the hearts of people to different kinds of soil. One unproductive soil is the stony ground (Luke 8:6, 13). Underlying a few inches of topsoil is a shelf of bedrock. The seed of truth falls into that ground and springs up quickly. It wilts just as quickly in the hot sun, however, because there is no depth of earth for the roots. I believe that the bedrock underlying the topsoil is stubbornness. No matter how much good seed of truth is planted in our hearts, if we allow an underlying stubbornness in our lives, we will be unstable under pressure.

Stubbornness is referred to by several terms in the Bible. In James 1 it is called "double-mindedness," and the apostle says that the double-minded man is like "a wave of the sea driven with the wind and tossed." He is "unstable in all his ways" (James 1:6-8). Our double-mindedness stubbornly returns to our *own* way even though we know it is at odds with *God's* way.

When our trouble comes from other people, we often think that if we can just get the other person to change, everything will stabilize. Unfortunately—or perhaps fortunately—we have no control over others. The only person we can control is ourself. It is crucial for us to understand that no decision of anyone else can destroy our inner man—our heart. We are the only ones who can destroy our hearts.

If we get bitter, angry, fearful, anxious, or hopeless, it is entirely our own doing. We have allowed self-centeredness to rule in our heart and contaminate it. Dealing with each of these "fevers" individually is outside the scope of this short study. What is important for us to understand initially, however, is that *the greatest danger is always the flesh*.[2]

Though other people may have created the wound, we are responsible for our reactions to it. There is no doubt that Bill has created Peggy's wound, but Peggy is responsible for her reaction to it. She can respond selfishly, thinking only of how Bill has betrayed her and made her life more difficult. Or she can respond like Christ and be concerned about the spiritual needs of other people—in this case, Bill's needs. It was Jesus who told us to love even our enemies. He said,

> *Love* your enemies, *bless* them that curse you, *do good* to them that hate you, and *pray* for them which despitefully use you, and persecute you (Matthew 5:44).

YOU'VE GOT TO BE KIDDING!

There is no doubt that responding to our trouble in a Christlike way is going to be tough to do. Loving, blessing, doing good to, and praying for those who mistreat us do not come naturally. In fact, they go against everything within our fleshly nature. But to give in to our selfishness will bring great danger into the situation.

Peggy knew reacting wrongly to the situation was dangerous. I hope by now you, too, see that to react in the flesh is dangerous. I outlined for Peggy the plan we shall look at in the next two chapters. It is God's plan for cleansing our responses of fleshliness so that the danger is removed.

---

[1]Peggy and Bill are not the real names of this couple. Their names and some of the details have been changed to protect their identity.

[2]For an extended account of a man who suffered wrongfully and yet had the proper response, read Genesis 37-50. It is the account of a Hebrew boy named Joseph, who was mistreated by his brothers, sold into slavery, falsely accused of attempted rape, and unjustly imprisoned. His proper responses, however, allowed him to be a great blessing to two nations and even to be the deliverer of the brothers who had sold him into slavery.

3

THE PLAN

RESCUING A CAT

Since the terrorist attacks on the World Trade Center and the Pentagon on September 11, 2001, we all have a new appreciation for our police and firefighting forces. We have heard stories of the heroic efforts of these men and women to save as many lives as possible during those awful hours following the attacks. These unsung heroes perform this service in small towns and large cities all over this nation every day of the year.

They have been trained to skillfully rescue people in times of disaster. It seems almost ludicrous to say, but *any firefighter who can rescue someone from the third story of a burning building using a ladder truck can easily rescue a cat in a tree*. We should certainly expect that if the fireman can deliver someone from great danger, he can also deliver someone from a lesser danger.

In the same way, the God who can rescue us from a crisis of staggering proportions can deliver us from lesser troubles as well.

OUR BIGGEST CRISIS

We must ask ourselves then, "What is the biggest crisis a man can face?" The average man on the street might answer, "Losing my family would be my biggest crisis." Others might respond that losing their health would be their greatest crisis. Jesus Himself told us what is the biggest crisis a man can face. He said,

> For what is a man profited, if he shall gain the whole world, and lose his own soul? Or what shall a man give in exchange for his soul? (Matthew 16:26).

Jesus' greatest concern for a man is that his soul should be rescued from eternal destruction in hell. Jesus spoke often of hell—more often than He spoke of heaven. He described it as a place of literal and everlasting torment.[1] He was so concerned that people not have to suffer in hell that

He Himself became a part of the most wonderful rescue plan of all time.

The interesting thought for you in this discussion of crises is that if you know how to be rescued from the greatest danger you could ever face—eternal separation from God because of your sin—you know how to be rescued from the dangers of whatever trial you are facing now. That brings us to the second truth on our "emergency checklist."

Truth #2: The gospel is always the answer.

A Crucial Question

Let me ask you a personal question. If you were to die today from a terminal illness or in some tragic accident and you were to stand before God, how would you answer God when He asked you this question: "Why should I let you into My heaven?"[2]

Some people might feel that because they have been deeply religious and have obeyed the Ten Commandments[3] most of the time, God should let them into heaven. Others might feel that because they have lived by the Golden Rule[4] and have been honest and moral in their dealings with others, they should be allowed to enter. They are saying essentially that God should allow them to enter heaven because they have been good in some way.

Jesus predicted that many people would come to Him on that day and would say exactly those things. He says that His reply to them will be, "I never knew you: depart from me, ye that [practice sin]" (Matthew 7:23). You see, no matter how many good things we have done, the factor that will keep us out of heaven is our sin.

The Bible makes it clear that "*all* have sinned, and come short of the glory of God" (Romans 3:23). That means that all of us have lived as if *we* are important and that God doesn't matter. We instinctively place ourselves first instead of God and turn to our "*own* way" (Isaiah 53:6).

Even our effort to get to heaven by being good shows our rebellion against God because He said that there is no way any of us can be good enough to merit heaven. Every one of us has broken His Ten Commandments—and have done so many times. He very clearly said that the "wages of sin is [eternal] death" (Romans 6:23). That means that all of us, because of our rebellion of going our own stubborn way in life, deserve the everlasting punishment of hell because of our mutiny against the Creator.

GOOD NEWS!

The good news for us is that eternal life—life in heaven with Jesus Christ forever—is not something we have to earn. *It is a gift!* Though "the wages of sin is [eternal] death; . . . the gift of God is eternal life through Jesus Christ our Lord" (Romans 6:23). That is good news because the Bible also tells us that it is "not by works of righteousness which we have done, but according to His mercy he saved us" (Titus 3:5). God is willing to mercifully give us a *gift* we cannot earn. He *wants* to give us eternal life. But that gift must be personally *received* by us.

The student center on the campus of Bob Jones University, where I minister, operates a lost and found area for the students. If the lost item has a name on it, the student center staff notifies the student to come to pick it up. If there is no name on it, the staff holds it for several weeks and then disposes of it or sells it for a small price at a lost and found sale. The staff is very willing to let the student have his property, but he must come by and show his identification card to claim it.

Salvation from the eternal punishment of our sins is available to everyone, but we, too, must personally claim it.

How can salvation be a free gift? Though it is free to us, it cost Jesus Christ everything. You see, our sins against God require that a penalty be paid. Sinning against our Creator is such a great offence that the only just penalty is eternal suffering and separation from God Himself in hell. Hell is the result of God's granting a man his request —"God, leave me alone." We may not realize it, but that is essentially what we say to God every time we reject His way and live life our own way. That is the bad news for the sinner.[5]

The good news is that God loves us and arranged for His own Son to live on this earth to pay the penalty for us. Though Jesus lived in a body like ours, He did not share our sinful and stubborn nature. He lived a sinless life in complete obedience to His Father while on the earth. He qualified—as a perfect sacrificial lamb—to die in our place. Look at these chilling but wonderful words from the Old Testament, which predicted the sacrificial death of Jesus Christ on the cross for us.

> He was wounded for *our* transgressions, he was
> bruised for *our* iniquities: the chastisement [for] *our*
> peace was upon him: and with his stripes *we* are
> healed. All we like sheep have gone astray; we have

turned everyone to his own way; and the Lord hath laid on him the iniquity of *us* all (Isaiah 53:5-6).

The apostle John states the same thing this way:

> For God so loved the world, that he gave his only begotten Son, that whosoever believeth in him should not perish, but have everlasting life. . . . He that believeth on him is not condemned: but he that believeth not is condemned already, because he hath not believed in the name of the only begotten Son of God (John 3:16, 18).

Jesus' sacrifice of His own blood as the eternal payment for anyone who would believe on Him satisfied the righteous anger of God against our mutiny. All that is left is for us to admit to God that we are indeed hell-deserving sinners, realize that Jesus died in our place and arose from the dead, and then accept the gift of eternal life from God. It is a simple plan—one that even a child can understand. A child will cry out for help to the person he believes will help him. A sinner who wants the gift of eternal life can come to Jesus Christ by praying a prayer like this:

Lord Jesus, I realize that I am a sinner. I have not obeyed You. I have gone my own way many times. Since You are perfect and Your heaven is perfect, I realize that even one sin would disqualify me from heaven.[6] I repent of my sin and ask Your forgiveness. I accept Your gift of eternal life. I want Your substitutionary death to be applied to my sin account.[7] Cleanse me from my sin and make me one of Your own children.[8] Thank You for loving me and for saving me.

Once you are a child of God, your *greatest* crisis is over. You may lose the whole world, but you will not lose your soul.

Now consider this: *If God knows how to rescue you from your greatest crisis, He certainly knows how to deliver you from any other crisis of life.* And as we shall see, if you know how to be rescued from your greatest crisis—eternal death—you already know how to be rescued from any lesser crisis of life. We'll look at that in some detail in the next chapter.

---

[1]For example, Jesus told the account of two men who actually lived. When both died, one went to heaven; the other went to hell. You can read about it yourself in Luke 16:19-31.

[2]If you are a born-again believer, do not skip over this brief chapter. Most believers do not recognize that "salvation" from this present crisis involves the same plan that gave them eternal life. Thus, they have trouble handling the temporal crises of life. Prayerfully reflect on this chapter even if you have been a Christian for some time. Its truths must become "front-burner" issues for you if you are to handle life well.

[3]Exodus 20:3-17.

[4]The Golden Rule: "Do unto others as you would have them do unto you" is a paraphrase of Jesus' statement in Matthew 7:12.

[5]Jesus Himself speaks of hell as a place of literal torment (Luke 16:19-31).

[6]James 2:10.

[7]II Corinthians 5:21.

[8]John 1:12.

4

THE APPLICATION

BACK TO THE CAT

I said in the last chapter that "any firefighter who can rescue someone from the third story of a burning building using a ladder truck can easily rescue a cat in a tree. . . . In the same way, the God who can rescue us from a crisis of staggering proportions can deliver us from lesser troubles as well."

As we have seen, our biggest crisis is the need for the salvation of our sinful souls. God, in His love, worked out a plan to rescue us from eternal destruction. That plan is called the gospel and is the pattern for every other kind of rescue God does for us. The next question is "How do we *apply* it to our suffering today?"

A View from a Wheelchair

Tim Mahler was a sophomore Bible major at Bob Jones University. It was summertime, and he was working for an electrical contractor in his hometown in Maine. While riding to the job site at 5:30 one morning, both Tim and his coworker, who was driving, fell asleep.

When the driver lost control of the car, Tim was thrown through the windshield, breaking his spinal column. The injury was between the fifth and sixth vertebrae. This left him with no voluntary movement or feeling from the bottom of his shoulders down. Tim became a quadriplegic.

When the doctors told Tim at age nineteen that he would be a quadriplegic, his life was not "devastated, derailed, or dead-ended"—to use Tim's own words. Why? Since Tim knew how God saved him from the dangers of his eternal crisis, he knew how God could save him from the dangers of his earthly crisis.

Tim did not grow emotionally numb, angry, or depressed or live for a period of time in denial. He was rescued from these dangers of the flesh the same way he was rescued from the dangers of eternal death when he first became a Christian.

LIVE THE CHRISTIAN LIFE
THE SAME WAY YOU GOT IT

Colossians 2:6 says, "As ye have therefore received Christ Jesus the Lord, so walk ye in him." This verse teaches that our initial salvation from sin is the pattern for our continued progress in being saved from our selfish tendencies. The gospel teaches us the pattern. Here are its basic components.

The gospel reveals man's condition. We saw in the last chapter that the Bible says we are all sinners. When we receive Jesus Christ as our Savior, we are forgiven for our sins and do not have to pay the eternal *penalty* of our sins, but we are not yet delivered from the *presence* of sin in our lives. The Bible teaches us that we still have within us the bent to live selfishly—to think of ourselves first. This inclination to think of ourselves first seems overwhelming at times—especially if we are in great pain.

The gospel reveals God's provision. Though our sin nature still remains with us, God has provided a solution to its domination: a relationship with Jesus Christ. The provisions we need to deal with our temptations to be angry, bitter, anxious, fearful, and despairing will not be found in programs that teach us to manage emotions or teach us how to relax and find answers deep within ourselves. Neither will the solution ultimately be in the comfort of other people or in principled living.

The only lasting and satisfying answer to life's problems will always be in increased intimacy with Jesus Christ. Any solution that does not put Jesus Christ center stage will be ineffective and will further complicate the problem.

We cannot be saved from eternal death by trusting in Jesus Christ *and* our good efforts. We cannot be saved by trusting Jesus Christ *and* the church. Neither can we be saved from the dangers of the fleshly responses to our present crises by anything that detracts from the centrality of Jesus Christ. Any comfort we receive or strategies we attempt must point us to Jesus Christ, who alone is our Savior. God's provision isn't a program or even a set of principles; it is a Person. Since the flesh is the greatest danger, the gospel—which puts Jesus Christ in the spotlight—is the only answer.

The gospel reveals man's responsibilities. Whether a firefighter is rescuing someone from a burning building or rescuing a cat from a tree, the basics are the same. First, set up the ladder. Second, climb up the ladder. Third, bring the person—or cat—down safely. Admittedly, there are differences between rescuing people from a burning building and rescuing a cat from a tree. But my point is that there are also very great similarities—as there are between being rescued from the dangers of hell's torment and being rescued from the dangers of selfish responses.

Man's responsibilities in salvation are first to turn from his sinful bent to trust himself to make life work. Self-centeredness is at the root of his problem. He must confess his mutiny against God and ask forgiveness.

Secondly, he must trust the provisions God has made available for his redemption. God has made salvation available to anyone who turns to Christ for forgiveness. The Bible message is "believe on the Lord Jesus Christ, and thou shalt be saved" (Acts 16:31).

In the same way, Tim turned in humble dependence to Jesus Christ for the inner strength he would need to live as a quadriplegic. He realizes daily that his circumstances are overwhelmingly against him. Left to his own self-centered ways, he would be bitter and discouraged. Listen to Tim's own words.

> During the first year after my injury, I didn't need
> to progress through the five stages of grief: shock, denial,

anger, guilt, and depression. Why? In part because I
had a competent medical staff attending to my physical
needs and dedicated parents, who daily provided me
support, but most importantly because my relationship
with God's Son had not been altered in any way
through this unanticipated incident.

Practically speaking, this meant that when everyone had left my bedside there was still someone
there—Christ—the one who promised that He by no
means would desert or abandon me (Hebrews 13:5).
When my body became spent, my emotions spongy,
and my thoughts shaken, I could rest on Christ, the
everlasting Rock, as the prophet Isaiah describes Him
(Isaiah 26:4), who provides lasting stability. . . .[1]

A life focused on Christ will not crumble in crisis. If we
have placed our trust in Jesus Christ—God's Son as our sin-
bearer and sole master—then we have entered into a special
relationship.

Tim's family relocated to Greenville, S.C., within a year
of his accident. He finished his undergraduate degree in
Bible from BJU and went on to complete a master's degree

in Bible as well. Since then he has traveled extensively, testifying of the wonderful grace of God, which is able to keep him not only from the dangers of eternal death but also from the dangers of daily spiritual defeat. He also ministers on the staff of his home church in Greenville.

Tim closes his testimony with these words,

Maybe . . . you are like David T., a 34-year-old quadruple amputee . . . , who is searching for a way to cope with his injury. He writes in a recent periodical, "I'm trying to grapple with whether spirituality can maybe compensate for the limbs, for the life I'm missing. I've gotten into the habit of going to the theology section of Barnes and Noble to buy books on Zen. . . . I'm trying to find some spiritual connection so I can deal with this life as it is, with this body, with this lump, as I call it. Maybe there will be a spiritual connection that will give me an answer."[2]

The answer for David and all of us . . . is a personal relationship with God's Son, Jesus Christ. Jesus Himself said in John 6:35, "I am the bread of life: he that cometh to me shall never hunger; and he that

believeth on me shall never thirst." I am here . . . to
testify to you . . . that a life *focused* on Christ will not
crumble in crisis because that life is complete.

The plan is easy to understand but is not always easy to
do because our self-centered ways cry out for relief on our
terms.

The plan is to acknowledge the *danger* of stubborn self-
centeredness in our pain. We must ask Jesus Christ Himself
for the grace—the divine help—to respond in a way that
provides us the *opportunity* to show how loving and powerful Jesus Christ is in our pain.

Listen to the testimony of another man—the apostle
Paul—who endured great physical affliction and found that
the grace—the divine help—of God was the solution to re-
moving the dangers of self-centeredness and to preparing
the opportunities to show how great his God was.

And lest I should [exalt myself] above measure
[because of] the abundance of the revelations [note:
God had used Paul to write over one half of the books
of the New Testament—a heady accomplishment],
there was given to me a thorn in the flesh, the messen-

ger of Satan to buffet me, lest I should be exalted above measure. For this thing I besought the Lord thrice, that it might depart from me [note: three times he asked God to remove the affliction]. And he said unto me, My grace is sufficient for thee: for my strength is made perfect in weakness. Most gladly therefore will I rather glory in my infirmities, that the power of Christ may rest upon me. Therefore I take pleasure in infirmities, in reproaches, in necessities, in persecutions, in distresses for Christ's sake: for when I am weak, then am I strong (II Corinthians 12:7-10).

Salvation from the danger of eternal death requires repentance—turning from sin—and it requires faith—turning toward God. Salvation from the dangers of anger, bitterness, anxiety, despair, and so forth in our pain requires the same thing—repentance for our stubborn self-centeredness, and faith—turning our face toward God for His help. Can you—like Tim Mahler—pray something like this?

Lord Jesus, I see how easy it is for me right now to think only of myself in my pain. I realize that my self-centeredness and stubbornness are the source of my

anger, bitterness, anxiety, fear, despair, and hopeless-
ness. Please forgive me for thinking that what I want is
the most important thing in the world. Your plan is
most important. I am turning to You for help. Teach me
what You want me to know about Yourself so that I can
show others that You are first in my life by the way I
respond. I want others to see that You are truly suffi-
cient for whatever happens to me.

We will have a hard time praying this, however, if we do
not have the same agenda that God has for us in our trial. If
we think our relief is the most important thing, while God
thinks our growth in fellowship with Jesus Christ is most
crucial, we will not weather the crisis well. The next chapter,
"The Goal," will take a look at God's agenda vs. our agenda
in our trial.

---

[1]From "Clemson Testimony" by Tim Mahler on www.notearsin-
heaven.com, a website dedicated to encouraging those who have
experienced great tragedy. Used with permission.

[2]"Disability and Spirituality" in *New Mobility,* Nov. 1999, p. 39.

5

THE GOAL

Emergencies have a way of defining what is truly important. EMS personnel at an automobile accident site will not think twice about cutting off a trouser leg on an expensive pair of pants to attend to a serious wound on a victim's leg. Though the trousers may have cost a great deal of money at one time, they are sacrificed readily in order to save the victim's leg.

The crises of life are designed by God to help put the components of life back into their proper perspective. We saw this clearly on September 11, 2001, when America was attacked. Many Americans who had not thought of God for months, or perhaps years, suddenly began to pray. Churches of every denomination were filled with mourners and with people who wanted to know what their religious leaders had to say to them at the time.

Times of national and personal crisis jolt us out of our daydreams, our obsessions with work, and our trivial pursuits of recreation and entertainment. They bring us face to face with the ultimate reality—God.

There is no reality more significant than the facts that God exists, that He made us, and that He made us for a very specific purpose. And since we were created with a free will, we are responsible for whether we live our lives to accomplish God's purpose for us.

As I dictate the words of this chapter on a portable recorder, I am heading south on a highway that will take me to my brother's house in Palm Springs, California. I have chosen this road because it will accomplish that purpose. I am in California to speak at a camp and am making this trip to visit my brother the day before the camp begins. If my purpose were to visit the Hoover Dam, I would be on a different road right now going a different direction. My goal determines which road I travel.

In the very same way, our goal for our life will determine the decisions we make daily. That brings us to the next truth for handling troubled times.

Truth #3: God's glory is always the goal.

The apostle Paul said, "Whether therefore ye eat, or drink, or whatsoever ye do, do all to the glory of God" (I Corinthians 10:31). That "whatsoever ye do" includes all the decisions of life—even those that are the responses to our suffering and pain. If glorifying God is the purpose of our lives, it will determine which "roads"—which right decisions—will bring us to that "destination."

FACING THE FIERY FURNACE

The Bible gives us a wonderful example of three men who in the face of death made choices that showed the greatness and worthiness of their God. Three Old Testament Hebrew men—Shadrach, Meshach, and Abed-nego—were commanded to bow and worship a golden image of the reigning king of Babylon, Nebuchadnezzar.[1]

They refused to bow to the image. By that act of defiance to the king's command, they showed that their God was first in their lives. If they had bowed to the statue, they would have demonstrated that preserving their *own* lives was the most important thing to them.

Our responses during times of great pressure and suffering will reveal whether we truly believe that God is the most important reality or whether we think *we* are the most significant factor in life.

Shadrach, Meshach, and Abed-nego refused to think of themselves first and were sentenced to die. They were thrown bound into a fiery furnace that had been heated seven times hotter than normal.

God did a miraculous thing for them and spared their lives. Not only did He keep them from being burned alive but He also sent a heavenly messenger—perhaps an Old Testament appearance of Jesus Christ Himself—to be with them in the furnace. Listen to the words of the astonished King Nebuchadnezzar to his associates on that day.

> Did not we cast three men bound into the midst
> of the fire? They answered and said unto the king,
> True, O king. [The king] answered and said, Lo, I see
> *four* men loose, walking in the midst of the fire, and
> they have no hurt; *and the form of the fourth is like the*
> *Son of God.*

This passage gives us some wonderful instruction for handling the "fiery furnaces" of our lives. First, it teaches us that we should always respond in a way that shows that God is more important than anything else to us. And it also teaches us that we should respond in such a way that others who watch us in our "fiery furnace" can see someone "like the Son of God" with us in the furnace of our trial.

In this way we can glorify God because it shows we esteem *Him* of highest value. We show that we are not living in a fantasy world where we imagine that the world revolves around *us*. The most significant factor of reality is that God towers above all things in great splendor and majesty.

Thinking like this runs contrary to our natural, fleshly nature. We normally like to promote ourselves, protect ourselves, and please ourselves. The irony of this is that selfishness is at the center of all of our unhappiness in life. God has so "wired" His universe that any response from man that shows Him to be first fills that man with the joy and peace he longs for.

This truth is what Jesus was talking about when He said,

If any man will come after me, let him deny himself, and take up his cross daily, and follow me. For

> whosoever will save his life shall lose it: but whosoever
> will lose his life for my sake, the same shall save it
> (Luke 9:23-24).

Self-centered goals will always bring us a great deal of unhappiness. Our goal must be to use every circumstance to show in some way that God is first. The result will be a lasting joy and peace no matter how difficult the circumstances.

BACK TO PEGGY AND BILL

Do you remember the story of Peggy, who discovered her husband's indulgences in internet pornography? Her main goal was to show how God was first in her life. She wanted to respond in such a way that Bill would see something of the grace and kindness, as well as the holiness, of God. She could have very easily responded in a self-centered way that would show nothing about her great God to her equally selfish husband. Had she done so, the situation could have escalated very quickly into the same kind of bloodbath they had experienced ten years earlier.

Peggy left my office determined to glorify God in her responses. She lovingly but firmly confronted Bill about how he was putting himself before Jesus Christ and others. The next day Bill came to my office to tell me how Peggy had graciously challenged him about his spiritual failure. He had asked her forgiveness and had already contacted his pastor, who promised to meet with him on a regular basis to disciple him out of his self-centered ways.

Bill was grieved at his sin but was also filled with great joy that his fellowship with God and with his wife was restored. His repentance also brought great joy to Peggy because she had seen once again the glory of God—His faithfulness, wisdom, power, and love.

WHAT IF IT GETS WORSE?

What if Bill's response had not been one of repentance? What if Bill had continued in his sin for many years? Or what if Peggy had been watching her husband's body waste away with cancer of the liver instead of watching his soul shrivel up due to the toxins of pornography? Could Peggy glorify God if the circumstances did not improve, but rather got worse?

It is important for us to understand that God is not glorified merely by miraculous recoveries and heart-warming times of repentance. He is glorified *any time* His people have responses that show He is first in their lives.

The patriarch Job demonstrated that God was first by his response to the loss of his family, farm, and health. He said, "Though he slay me, yet will I trust in him" (Job 13:15). "The Lord gave, and the Lord hath taken away; blessed be the name of the Lord. In all this Job sinned not, nor charged God foolishly" (Job 1:21-22). Though Job eventually got his health and his farm back, he never saw his children brought back to life.

But I Am So Weak!

If you have read this far in our study together, you may be saying to yourself, "I see how all of this is true, and I genuinely would like to respond the way you are describing, but I am so weak. I don't have the strength to respond rightly, especially over the long haul."

If this is the genuine attitude of your heart, I have even more good news for you! Jesus taught in His first sermon that this kind of weakness and humility qualifies you for His help. In the section of that sermon we call the Beatitudes, He said that His blessing would be upon

- "the poor in spirit"—those who are spiritually bankrupt.

- "they that mourn"—those who grieve over their sinfulness and weakness.
- "the meek"—those willing to be governed by God and others.
- "they which do hunger and thirst after righteousness"—those who are spiritually thirsty.

The apostle Peter echoes the same thing when he tells us, "God resisteth the proud [i.e., stubborn], and giveth grace [i.e., divine help] to the humble" (I Peter 5:5).

When we humble ourselves before God, acknowledging that we need Him, and do not stubbornly insist on our own way, He responds to us by giving us divine help. That help comes in the form of an *increased desire* to do His will and *increased power* to perform it (Philippians 2:13).

During times of great suffering, our desire to do right can diminish, and we can think we do not have the strength to carry on. At these times especially, we need an increase of His grace.

WE ARE NEVER TOO WEAK TO BOW

The beauty of God's plan is that no matter how weak and feeble we become, we can always humble ourselves before Him. Fortunately, we do not have to do something great and powerful to get God's help. If that were the case, we would *never* be able to get His help.

It is easy for us in times of great pain and suffering to lose sight of our goal to show that God is first, especially when the pain and suffering drag on for an extended period of time. It is important during these prolonged times of difficulty to be reminded of what our goal is. If we lose sight of our goal, it is easy for us to lose our way in the darkness.

It is hard for us to understand, however, why God should be first if we do not know Him well. In the next two chapters we will explore some of the wonderful aspects of our God. Since it is hard to trust people we do not know well, we must increase in our knowledge of God.

The time of crisis is the time to pray something like this.

> *Lord Jesus, I realize that during this time of pain I am especially tempted to think of myself. I realize, however, that this is a marvelous opportunity to put You and others first, even as You put us first when You died on the cross to pay the penalty for our sins. Please use this time to make me more like You. May others see You here in the fiery furnace with me as they watch my life. Give me the daily strength and help I will need to keep*

*my eyes focused on the goal of glorifying You in my
trial. Please help me to respond properly for the sake of
Your glory.*

As long as the trial remains, we will have to make this
the daily cry of our hearts. We will receive in return a wonderful peace and a satisfying joy when *God's glory is always
the goal.*

---

[1]See Daniel 3 for the details of this amazing account.

6

THE DILEMMA

BOB'S SQUAD CAR

Anumber of years ago one of our graduates who serves on a municipal police force invited me to a certain high-crime area of his city. We approached one intersection in a run-down residential area. A gang of young men were congregating in the middle of the street in front of us. As we approached the group, the men moved out of the way to let us through, scowling at us as we passed. Bob knew most of them by name—and they knew Bob. I am glad I could not hear the comments they made to us as we passed by.

I would never want to drive into that part of that city, even in broad daylight, in my own car. I felt quite safe that afternoon, however, riding in Bob's squad car. I was surrounded by bulletproof glass and heavy gauge metal. A shotgun was very visible, strapped to the dashboard of the car. Bob had an impressive array of communication radios at his disposal as well as his own personal firearm. An awareness of Bob's resources put my natural fears to rest.

In the same way, the answer for the fears we experience in times of crisis is an increased awareness of the nature of our God. In this chapter and the next, I want to briefly take you on a tour of God's "squad car." I want to survey the powers that He has at His disposal, which He will use for our benefit and for His glory.

Sometimes people say, "I have a hard time trusting God." The truth may be that they are refusing to trust Him because trusting means giving up control of their lives in some area. We have already seen the danger of our self-centered ways. Another reason they might have a "hard time" trusting God is that they do not know Him very well.

TRUSTING STRANGERS

Suppose a man you have never met stops you in a mall. He tells you that if you will loan him $50 and give him your name, address, and phone number, he will gladly pay you back when he gets his paycheck in a couple of days. Even the most compassionate of us would probably not give the stranger $50. And we would all think twice before giving out our name, address, and phone number to someone we do not know. We don't know what he would do with that information. The simple fact is that we don't trust people we don't know.

What if, on the other hand, the man who stops you is someone close to you and whom you respect highly—your brother or your father—who has absent-mindedly left his wallet at home. If you have the $50, you will likely loan him the money. He has proven himself trustworthy in your past dealings with him. He has consistently shown in your previous experiences with him that he had your best interests at heart when he dealt with you—hence, your great respect for him. You are very willing to help someone whom you regard so highly.

THE DILEMMA

The application for many of us is all too pointed and painful. We have to admit that often we have a hard time trusting God because we really don't consider Him trustworthy. To us He looks more like a wolf among the sheep—making life miserable for us—than a Good Shepherd, who is willing to give His life for the sheep. This is our dilemma: Whom will we trust?

We may have formed our view of God from hearsay—what others have told us about Him. Or our view of Him may be skewed by situations that did not turn out the way *we* wanted them resolved, and we have blamed God for our misfortune.

Our sinful natures are clones of Satan's own nature. Our flesh, like Satan, is deceitful.[1] Satan keeps our heart under his rule by scandalizing God. He does everything he can to make God look bad and to make himself look good. Satan is so effective in his strategy that he has temporarily taken over the loyalty of virtually the whole world.

TRUST DECISIONS

The apostle Paul accurately calls Satan "the god of this world," who "hath blinded the minds of them which believe not" (II Corinthians 4:4). In every circumstance of life, we have a trust decision to make. Will we believe what *God* has said about our situation, or will we believe what *our own heart* tells us about our situation—skewed by its natural bent to mimic Satan?

This is why the Bible speaks so much about faith. We may think that the key factor is the amount of our faith. Scripture indicates that we always have enough faith. Our problems result from placing our faith in the wrong person.

When the Bible speaks about our having faith, it refers to having faith *in God*. This is what is meant when the Bible says, "the just [i.e, the ones who are righteous before God because they have experienced God's salvation from sin] shall live by faith" (Romans 1:17).

We cannot make any decisions without believing somebody. The test of our spiritual life is "*whom* are we believing with our faith—God or our own heart?"

A Christian facing surgery for cancer, heart problems, or other serious matters has a trust decision to make. If he trusts *God*, his heart responds in a manner something like this:

> *Heavenly Father, I do not know what kind of outcome You have for me in this surgery. I know that my own heart would like to insist that this operation completely solve my physical problem. But I know that You might have other plans.*

> *In Your wisdom You might have already decided that it is best that my suffering continue. You might even have chosen that I not survive the surgery and that I should enter into Your presence sooner than any of us here on this earth had thought.*

I know You love me. You have told me that since You "spared not [Your] own Son, but delivered him up for us all, how shall [You] not with him also freely give us all things?"[2] You proved Your love to me when You sacrificed Your own wonderful Son, Jesus Christ, to take care of my greatest need—the salvation of my soul. I won't doubt Your love in this matter. The evidence of Your love for me is too great.

My heart could easily be filled with fears right now, so I am humbling myself before You and asking that You give me the grace You promised so that I will not deny Your trustworthiness by giving in to fears. Help me to keep my focus on You—my Strengthener and Redeemer, my Good Shepherd.

NEW TESTAMENT TROUBLE

The apostles of the early church in Jerusalem experienced particularly difficult times because their message of salvation in Jesus Christ cut cross-grain to the accepted religious thought of the day. They were regularly summoned before government officials for their preaching and were flogged or imprisoned. Notice this account in Acts 4:23-29 of their response after one such encounter. I want you to especially notice their high view of God and of His Son, Jesus Christ.

> And being let go, [Peter and John] went to their own company, and reported all that the chief priests and elders had said unto them. And when [the church] heard that, they lifted up their voice to God with one accord, and said,

> *Lord, thou art God, which hast made heaven, and earth, and the sea, and all that in them is:* who by the mouth of thy servant David hast said, Why did the heathen rage, and the people imagine vain things? The kings of the earth stood up, and the rulers were gathered together against the Lord, and against his Christ. [In other words, "You predicted that the unbelieving world would act this way toward Your Son."]

> For of a truth against thy holy child Jesus, whom thou hast anointed, both Herod and Pontius Pilate, with the Gentiles, and the people of Israel, were gathered together, *for to do whatsoever thy hand and thy counsel determined before to be done.*

> And now, Lord, behold their threatenings: and
> grant unto thy servants, that with all boldness they may
> speak thy word.

These first-century believers readily acknowledged that their God was the powerful Creator and could do whatever He wished to do in the affairs of men. They didn't insist that their *own* agenda be fulfilled. They asked only that they would be able to testify to the greatness of their God with boldness even when they faced persecution. God answered their prayer, for we find these words in verse 33:

> And with great power gave the apostles witness of
> the resurrection of the Lord Jesus: and great grace was
> upon them all.

Only by having the same view of God as these early apostles can we sincerely pray the Lord's Prayer.[3] The words I have added in brackets help clarify the meaning of this well-known model prayer.

> Our Father which art in heaven, Hallowed be thy
> name. Thy kingdom come. Thy will be done [through

me] in earth, as it is [accomplished by your heavenly servants] in heaven.

These verses teach us that we will not be ready to ask God to accomplish whatever His will is in our lives here on earth if we do not "hallow" His name.

The word "hallowed" means to be especially honored and exalted in such a way that sets Him high above—separate—from all other beings. It means to view with great respect and dignity. As we saw earlier, it is much easier to trust someone whom we highly respect since *every decision is a trust decision*—it reveals whom we trust.

So how is it that we can gain this high view of God? How can we believe rightly—make the right trust decisions—about God? We will attempt a more complete answer to that question in the next chapter. We will take some time to look more closely at His "squad car"—the resources He has at His disposal to use on our behalf.

---

[1]Jeremiah 17:9; John 8:44.

[2]Romans 8:32.

[3]Matthew 6:9-13.

7

THE HIGH TOWER

ESCAPE FROM THE TOWER

Shirley and Steve—not their real names—sat across the table from my wife and me as Shirley told her story. She was on an upper floor of the second World Trade Center tower when the first tower was hit by Islamic terrorists in a commercial airliner. She and her work associates were able to escape unharmed minutes before the first tower collapsed. They along with hundreds of others ran away from the site and kept on walking. Their only goal: to get out of the city and let their loved ones know they were alive. Though the twin towers would soon collapse, Shirley was still protected by a far more secure unseen tower—the God of heaven.

When David faced danger, he was eager to run into that Strong Tower. Here are his words:

> The Lord is my rock, and my fortress, and my deliverer; my God, my strength, in whom I will trust; my [shield], and the horn of my salvation, and my *high tower* (Psalm 18:2).

> Hear my cry, O God; attend unto my prayer. From the end of the earth will I cry unto thee, when my heart is overwhelmed: lead me to the rock that is higher than I. For thou hast been a shelter for me, and a *strong tower* from the enemy (Psalm 61:1-3).

> Blessed be the Lord my [rock], . . . my [lovingkindness], and my fortress; my *high tower,* and my deliverer; my shield, and he in whom I trust (Psalm 144:1-2).

ESCAPE *TO* THE TOWER

High towers—like the World Trade Center towers—are dangerous places to be during an emergency. But as these verses teach us, God is a strong tower—our safest place of refuge during an emergency.

This theme of running *to* God during times of crisis is a frequent theme in the Bible and is captured in the fourth and final truth for times of trouble.

Truth #4: God Himself is always enough.

Since America has experienced the tragedy of the World Trade Center attacks, people are quite ready to evacuate a tall building at the first hint of threat. Buildings that were at one time thought to be entirely safe are viewed as possible deathtraps now.

Unfortunately, many people have as skeptical a view of God as they do of tall buildings. Instead of running to Him in times of danger, they run away from Him. As I mentioned in the last chapter, they do this because they do not know Him well.

When my wife is counseling women who are going through uncertain times, she reminds them of an important truth: When there are things that you do not know about your life's situation, you must focus on the things that you do know about your God.

It is very easy for any of us when facing uncertain times to feel that our heart could rest if only we knew

- whether we really have cancer.
- whether our spouse is really being unfaithful.
- whether our teen is really doing drugs.
- whether our investments will be there when retirement time comes.

Consequently, we often go on relentless searches for the answers to those questions, seeking rest for our heart. The trouble with that strategy is that we often cannot find out the answers we want until it is too late to do anything about them. How then can our heart find rest in times of trouble?

We must increase our knowledge of God Himself—the one who is controlling all the factors of our life in His sovereignty.[1] We may not be able to see exactly what He is doing or how He will make something turn out, but if we know Him well, our heart can rest.

COURAGE TO FACE A BULLY

When our daughters were young, a neighborhood boy occasionally intimidated the younger children with his threats and physical force. The back door of our apartment led out to the play area for the apartment complex in which

64

we lived. One day I stood at the back door of our apartment watching the following scene unfold.

Our oldest daughter was playing in the sandbox when "the bully" came out of his apartment and headed for the sandbox. My daughter, upon seeing the boy approach, immediately got out of the sandbox and headed for the back door of our apartment. She took a few steps toward home when she spotted me looking out the screen door.

I could almost see the tiny gears turning in her head as she stopped in her tracks, paused for a moment, and then boldly returned to the sandbox. Once situated again in the sand, she periodically turned to see if I was still standing at the door. As long as I was there, she felt at peace—even in the presence of the neighborhood bully.

Her heart was at rest because she knew that her daddy was bigger than the threatening boy. She also knew that I loved her enough to rescue her if she were threatened in some way. In the same way, David's heart was immediately put at rest when he reminded himself that God was stronger than any of his enemies and that His God loved him enough to rescue him.

THE CRISIS REVEALS WHAT WE KNOW

If our hearts are not at rest when trouble comes, it is because we do not realize how powerful and wise God is or because we do not realize how much He loves us. It is not possible in this brief book to present a thorough study of God. Instead, I shall list several passages of Scripture that you can meditate upon to help you see the greatness and the goodness of our wonderful God. If you do not have a personal plan for meditation, you may want to use the MAP Method outlined for you in the appendix.

God is unlimited in His power:	Ephesians 1:19-20; Ephesians 3:20; Luke 1:37; Jeremiah 32:17
God is unlimited in His wisdom:	Psalm 18:30; Romans 11:33; Colossians 2:3; Psalm 147:5; I Corinthians 1:25
God is unlimited in His love:	Jeremiah 31:3; Romans 5:8; Romans 8:35-39

The Crisis Reveals What We Are

Sometimes extended personal trouble results in a physical crisis of some kind. We may experience stomach disorders, chronic pain, or some other abnormality.

Before the crisis we may not have been eating, exercising, or resting adequately. The crisis reveals a weakened physical condition when we are put under extra pressure.

Our spiritual lives are much the same way. We may experience great despair, heightened anxiety, anger, or bitterness when we face a time of trouble. These discomforts reveal that we have not been adequately taking care of our spiritual life. We need *more* personal meditation on the Word of God, *more* time in prayer with our great God, *more* exposure to the faithful preaching of the Bible, and *more* encouragement and fellowship with God's people.

A crisis reveals what we are made of spiritually. If we have a high biblical view of God through the consistent study of His Word, we will run to our Strong Tower, and our hearts will rest because *God Himself is always enough!*

What You Can Do Now

I hope you will use this time of crisis to more earnestly study your Bible to learn more about our great God. If you

67

are too ill physically to study your Bible, call your pastor or some spiritually mature friend and ask him to read the Bible to you.

If you are bedridden or confined to your house, purchase some recordings of good preaching. You can also purchase recordings of good Christian music and of someone reading the Bible.[2] All of these resources are means to help you learn more of our great God and to remind you again of truths you already know but may have forgotten in your time of trouble.

Keeping your mind focused on spiritual things during a crisis is of vital importance. Listen to the apostle Peter's instructions to his suffering congregation.

> Gird up the loins of your mind, be sober[minded],
> and [fix your hope on] the grace that is to be brought
> unto you at the revelation of Jesus Christ (I Peter 1:13).

"Gird up the loins of your mind" means to prepare your mind for action. Peter is saying that a time of crisis is no time for sloppy thinking. That is why it is important for us in times of crisis to be getting an increased dose of the Bible and of books and recordings that will teach us to think biblically.

It is also a time to fix our hope on what God is going to do for us in the future when we all will stand in His presence and will be delivered from the suffering and pain of this world. In the meantime, Peter tells us to continue to "grow in grace, and in the knowledge of our Lord and Saviour Jesus Christ" (II Peter 3:18).

You will find the Lord to be a Strong Tower when you get to know Him better. May you use this time of trouble to discover more about Him. You will one day be able to testify with great joy and peace that *God Himself is always enough!*

---

[1]That God is sovereign simply means that, as the reigning King over all the earth and heavens, He is directly superintending every aspect of our lives (Psalm 103:19).

[2]Sermon recordings, recordings of Scripture reading, and recordings of solid Christian music are available from the Bob Jones University Campus Store (1-800-242-1927 or www.bju.edu).

TAKE TIME TO REFLECT

The following questions are designed to help you think more carefully about the truths presented in each chapter of this book. Write out your answers. You will think through them more clearly if you write them out.

CHAPTER ONE—THE CRISIS

1. Describe the crisis you are facing right now.
2. Circle the words that describe your crisis:

   temporary   permanent
   caused by you   caused by others

CHAPTER TWO—THE DANGER

1. If you respond to this crisis in a selfish way, how can you "further infect the wound"?

2. In what ways do you find yourself being stubborn in this crisis?

CHAPTER THREE—THE PLAN

1. How would you answer the question "If you were to die today from a terminal illness or in some tragic accident, and you were to stand before God, how would you answer God when He asks you this question: 'Why should I let you into My heaven?'"

2. Have you ever realized that you are a sinner under the just condemnation of God and asked Jesus Christ to forgive your sins and be your Savior? If so, describe when that event took place.

CHAPTER FOUR—THE APPLICATION

1. What kept Tim Mahler from becoming bitter at God and at the driver of the car when Tim became a quadriplegic?

2. Salvation from the dangers of anger, bitterness, anxiety, despair, and so forth requires that we repent of our stubborn self-centeredness and that we turn to God in faith, asking Him to give us His help. Have you done that in this crisis? If so, explain when you did that and what you said to God.

CHAPTER FIVE—THE GOAL

1. How can you demonstrate to others that God is the most important person in your situation right now?

2. No matter how weak we get in our time of trouble, we can always humble ourselves before God and get more of His grace. Describe a time when you recently did this during your crisis.

CHAPTER SIX—THE DILEMMA

1. What makes your crisis especially difficult at this time?

2. Since every decision we make is a trust decision, whom do your decisions reveal you are trusting most—your *own* understanding or God? Describe one such decision.

CHAPTER SEVEN—THE STRONG TOWER

1. Which of the three aspects of God—His wisdom, His power, or His love—do you need help in understanding more fully? Explain why you chose that particular aspect.

2. What are you doing to "gird up the loins of your mind" [i.e., prepare your mind for action] during this time of crisis? If you are not doing anything substantial toward that end, what could you be doing to better prepare your mind to think biblically during this time?

How to Meditate: The MAP Method

Find a portion of Scripture relevant to your problem or find one that deals with a Bible truth you wish to master. Always meditate on Scripture that God's Spirit "highlights" as you are reading His Word.

Memorize the Passage

Memorizing often occurs automatically if the passage is studied intensely enough in the next step. During a temptation or a trial, you must know *exactly* what God has said *word for word*. Merely having a general idea about what is right is not enough when dealing with the deceptive nature of your own heart. A man who cannot remember God's exact words is in danger of leaning to his "own understanding" (Proverbs 3:5).

Many people memorize verses by writing the first letter of each word in a verse. For example, Psalm 119:105 says, "Thy word is a lamp unto my feet, and a light unto my path." The first letters are

T w i a l u m f, a a l u m p.

The first letter of each word (include the punctuation just as it appears in the text) gives enough of a prompt so that you can recall the word, but since the whole word is not present, you do not find yourself merely *reading* the words mindlessly.

ANALYZE THE PASSAGE

Study the passage, asking the Holy Spirit to give you a thorough understanding of its message. You can do an *intensive* study on the passage by listing the major words of the verses and then using an English dictionary to find out the meaning for each word. If possible, look up each word in a Greek or Hebrew dictionary or check the meaning of each word in *Strong's Exhaustive Concordance*. Once you are sure of each word's meaning, put the passage in your own words (i.e., paraphrase it). A more *extensive* study would involve using a commentary or good study Bible to help you understand more about who wrote the passage, to whom it was written, and why. Most importantly, pray that God will illumine your understanding. Ask Him to teach you what He wants you to know from the Scriptures.

PERSONALIZE THE PASSAGE

Plan concrete changes in your life that are consistent with your understanding of the passage. Such plans would include schedules, steps, and details. Ask yourself, "When have I failed to obey this truth in the past? When am I likely to meet a temptation again? What should be the godly response the next time I am tempted?" Think through this "game plan" *thoroughly* and *in advance* of the next temptation. Use the passage in a personal prayer to God. For example, a person meditating on James 4:1-11 may begin a prayer this way: "Lord, you tell me here in James 4:1 that the conflict I am having with John is the result of my own lusts—my desires to have something *my* way. I know that isn't pleasing to You. Instead of responding in anger to John, I need Your help and grace, which You promised in James 4:6 when you said that You resist the proud but give grace to the humble. Help me to humble myself instead of proudly insisting on my way. I want to allow You to lift me up in Your time. . . ."

TRUTHS FOR TIMES
OF TROUBLE

Feel free to duplicate the following card for your personal use. Please photocopy it as it appears below, including the copyright notice.

TRUTHS FOR TIMES OF TROUBLE

The greatest danger is always the flesh.

The gospel is always the answer.

God's glory is always the goal.

God Himself is always enough.

ADDITIONAL RESOURCES

If you desire biblical help during your time of trouble, you may contact Bob Jones University for a list of Bible-preaching churches in your area. To obtain such assistance contact the Office of Extension Ministries at BJU by calling 864-242-5100, extension 3850.

We hope this book has been a blessing to you. If you are interested in other resources written from a sound biblical perspective, please call BJU Press for a free catalog at 1-800-845-5731 or see www.bjup.com.

Changed into His Image

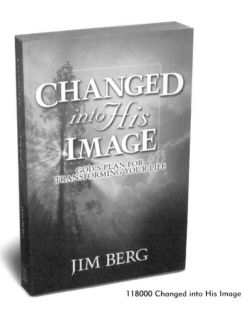

118000 Changed into His Image

In this inspirational book, Jim Berg presents
God's plan for lasting change and spiritual growth.

003582 Basics for Believers

Back to Basics

A valuable handbook for—

seasoned believers
discipling and encouraging others

new believers
desiring to grow spiritually

seekers
inquiring about faith in Christ
and the Christian walk

To order, call
1.800.845.5731
BJU PRESS

THE BIBLICAL COUNSELING SERIES

AN INTRODUCTION TO BIBLICAL COUNSELING

- What is biblical counseling?
- Who should counsel?
- The counseling process
- Utilizing homework
- How a believer changes and grows
- Dealing with issues of fear and anger
- Answering the self-esteem issue

COUNSELING ISSUES

- Anxiety and stress issues—includes biblical examination of panic disorders, phobias, obsessive-compulsive behavior, and psychosomatic illnesses

- Depression issues—includes a biblical look at manic-depressiveness and perfectionism
- Principles of biblical communication
- Dealing with sleep disorders
- Working with counselee's medication and physician
- Videotaped role-play case studies

CRISIS COUNSELING I

- Elements of crisis counseling
- The crisis of suicide
- The crisis of childhood sexual abuse—ten hours on how God gives "Beauty for Ashes"; offers help in understanding nature of abuse and biblical help for overcoming effects of abuse

CRISIS COUNSELING II

- The crisis of addiction: life-dominating sins—presents a biblical view of sin; help for working with eating disorders, drugs, and alcohol
- The crisis of immorality—teaches a biblical view of sex; gives help for dealing with pornography, homosexuality, adultery, etc.

Premarital Counseling

- Overview of the premarital counseling process—features a suggested multi-session program
- God's goals for marriage
- Biblical communication and problem solving
- Finances, sex, and in-laws
- Syllabus—includes nearly forty pages of inventories, questionnaires and projects for use with an engaged couple

Family Counseling

- Marriage and family content issues—includes a strategy for helping family members come to biblical reconciliation
- Marriage and family process issues—includes how to "unpack" the complex problems involved in order to get to the heart issues in each family member's life
- Marriage and family crisis issues—includes dealing with the growing problem of wife abuse and provides biblical answers for helping both the wife and the abusing husband

———————————————

This video series by Jim Berg can be ordered through the Extended Education division of BJU. Call 1-888-BJ-EXT-ED or see Extended Education at www.bju.edu.